WESTMINST

The Collegiate Church of St Peter, Westminster

———— Contents ————

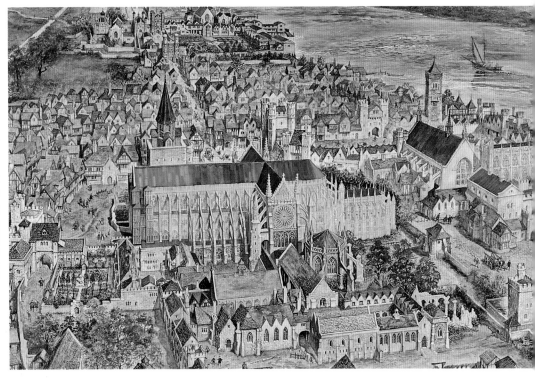

▲ Westminster in 1585, an artist's impression by Peter Jackson.

L egend has it that a church was first founded on the site of Westminster Abbey by Sebert, king of the East Saxons (died AD616) at the instigation of Mellitus, the first Bishop of London. The first religious foundation that we can be sure of was that of St Dunstan, a later Bishop. In the 960s, on an island in the Thames, he set up a Benedictine abbey. Very little is known about the building except that it stood not far from where the west door is now. Before long it was succeeded by a great monastery created by King Edward the Confessor (1042–66) on an adjacent site. Its focal point was a church, dedicated to St Peter, similar in area to the present building and built in the Norman French (Romanesque) style. The new church was hurriedly consecrated in late December 1065, just a few days before King Edward died. His remains still rest in the chapel which bears his name at the east end of the abbey.

The king built a palace nearby, in this one plan cementing bonds between Church and State which still continue. From the 14th to the 16th centuries, parliaments met in both the Chapter House and the refectory of the abbey. During this same period were buried most of the kings and queens whose tombs we see in the abbey today.

Less than 200 years after the first abbey's completion Henry III, in keeping with the religious zeal of the times, determined to replace it with something on a much grander scale. The old abbey was progressively demolished and replaced from the east end. Nothing of the old church now remains. Only in parts of the monastic buildings around the cloister does any Norman work still survive. The new abbey, although of similar area, was to be taller, lighter and more spacious – using better stone, mainly a greenish-grey sandstone from Reigate 37 kilometres (23 miles) away, with limestone from Caen in Normandy and pillars of polished Purbeck stone from Dorset. The master mason – architect in today's terms – was Henry de Reyns.

The style of the new Gothic church owed much to the style of contemporary French cathedrals – the apse with its radiating chapels, the tall windows and wall arcades of those chapels, the rose windows and wonderful flying buttresses. The outstanding French feature is the soaring height of the roof (32m/103ft) in relation to the narrow width of the nave and chancel (11m/35ft). However, the long nave and broad transepts are thoroughly English, as are the elaborate mouldings of the arches, the sculptured decoration and the use of polished Purbeck stone.

◀ St Edward the Confessor, as depicted in one of the early 20th-century nave windows by Sir Ninian Comper. ④

Many years of laborious but erratic progress followed as work on the nave continued westward (see pages 4–5). It is important to remember that the abbey we see today is not as medieval pilgrims to the Confessor's shrine would have seen it. They would have been confronted by exuberant colour everywhere – walls and vaulting covered with pictures and patterns in vibrant red, blue and gold. Tombs were encrusted with jewels and adorned with precious relics.

The nave was completed in 1517, the year that Martin Luther first lit the fires of Reformation. In 1540 the Abbot of Westminster surrendered his monastery to be dissolved. The Confessor's shrine was torn down and despoiled, statues destroyed and any forms of adornment abandoned.

From 1540 to 1550 the abbey became a cathedral in a newly created diocese of Westminster. The accession of Mary I in 1556 saw a community of monks re-established. Its brief existence was terminated in 1560 when Elizabeth I's Royal Charter designated the abbey as a collegiate church with a dean and a chapter of 12 canons.

The building was destined to retain its unfinished look for a further 200 years. Only in 1745 was the building as we know it today completed when the western towers were finished to the design of Sir Christopher Wren.

By the time of King Henry's death in 1272 the quire, sanctuary, transepts and some bays of the nave were complete, grafted incongruously onto the lower Norman nave. This state of affairs lasted for over a century, for there was no more money. Even to reach this stage, Henry had been forced to reclaim and pawn jewels that he had donated to adorn Edward the Confessor's shrine!

▼ A section of the Bayeux Tapestry showing mourners carrying the body of King Edward the Confessor to the newly completed abbey church. This is the only surviving pictorial evidence of the Norman abbey's appearance.

THE NAVE

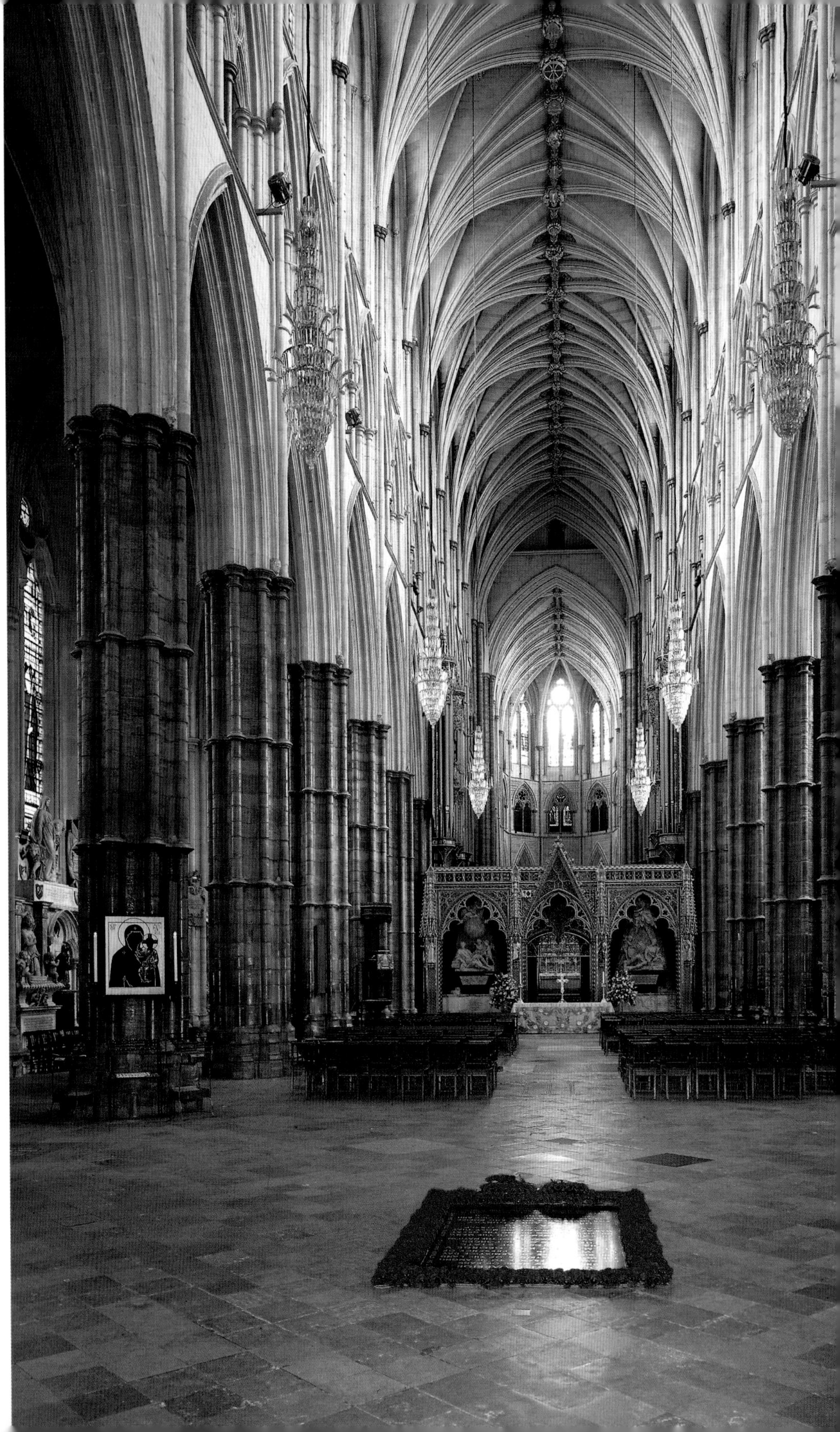

◄ The nave from the west door. The very French proportions of a 3:1 ratio of height to width are evident. The chandeliers are of crystal glass from Waterford, Ireland. Each chandelier weighs 127 kg and contains 500 pieces of glass. They were presented by the Guinness family in 1965 to mark the abbey's 900th anniversary. ③

To the right of the west door as one enters is St George's Chapel, sometimes called the Warrior's Chapel. In its time it has served as the venue for the abbey's consistory court, and later as the baptistry. In 1932 it was reordered to the design of Sir Ninian Comper and dedicated by the Prince of Wales, later Edward VIII, to men and women killed in World War I. The Union flag that hangs there was used by an army chaplain throughout that war as an altar cloth and to cover the bodies of soldiers killed in action.

The same flag was used in 1920 to cover the coffin of the Unknown Warrior, whose grave nearby commemorates the many thousands killed in World War I who were buried without ever being identified. The soil within the grave is French, the coffin is English oak and the slab is of Belgian marble.

▼ The Tomb of the Unknown Warrior. ③

▲ One of the dramatic icons in the nave. These are the work of the Russian painter Sergei Federov and were introduced into the abbey in 1994. ③

Between this grave and the west door is a simple memorial stone bearing the words 'Remember Winston Churchill' in honour of the famous statesman and prime minister (1874–1965). On the north side of the nave are eight windows designed by Sir Ninian Comper which depict kings and abbots who played some part in the building of the abbey. The one showing King Henry V (the seventh eastward) includes at the bottom that famous Lord Mayor, Dick Whittington, and his equally famous cat.

The magnificent nave of Henry III's church represented long years not just of physical toil on the part of the abbey monks, but of great efforts to raise the necessary funds to complete all 12 bays. The nave was begun towards the end of Henry's long reign (1216–72). Five bays were completed by the time of his death.

A start on the remaining western bays was not made until 1376 under Abbot Litlyngton. To his credit, the mason of the time, Henry de Yevele, kept faithfully to Henry de Reyns' now outmoded designs, but work proceeded only when funds were available. Thus it was not until around 1509 that the nave's basic structure was finished, with decoration and glazing continuing for another eight years. Between 1698 and 1745 Sir Christopher Wren and his successors completed the west end. In 1735, the great west window was glazed to the designs of Sir James Thornhill, who had painted the dome of Wren's great cathedral, St Paul's.

THE SCREEN, NORTH TRANSEPT & NORTH AMBULATORY

The screen separating the nave from the quire is the fourth to have stood here. It was designed by Edward Blore and erected in 1833–34. Only the wrought-iron gates survive from an earlier construction. Against the screen are two monuments, both designed by William Kent and sculpted by Michael Rysbrack. On the left is commemorated Sir Isaac Newton, the famous scientist; on the right James, 1st Earl Stanhope, a soldier and statesman.

Before the time of Queen Elizabeth I (reigned 1558–1603) it was mainly royalty or members of the monastic community that were buried in the abbey (with notable exceptions such as Chaucer, the great medieval poet). After 1560 when the abbey became a collegiate church the way was open for many more people to be laid to rest here. Today, around 3,500 people are known to be buried within the precincts.

Among those commemorated in the north quire aisle are Charles Darwin (1809–82), the naturalist who first propounded the theory of evolution, buried near Newton; also William Wilberforce (1759–1833) the reforming MP who campaigned tirelessly and successfully for the abolition of slavery in the British Empire. The composer Henry Purcell (1659–95), one of the abbey's greatest organists, is also buried here, near where the organ was once sited. His grave was the first of many memorials to British composers, among them Elgar, Vaughan Williams, Walton and Britten.

The north transept is known as Statesmen's Aisle, for here are memorials to famous British politicians of three centuries. William Pitt, later 1st Earl of Chatham (1708–78), was the first prime minister to be interred here. Others buried or commemorated include Palmerston (1784–1865), Disraeli (1804–81), Gladstone (1809–98)

▶ A monument against the screen commemorates the famous physicist, philosopher and mathematician, Sir Isaac Newton (1642–1727), who is buried here. Above is a globe showing constellations and signs of the zodiac. ⑥

◀ A statue of Benjamin Disraeli in that part of the north transept known as Statesmen's Aisle. ⑨

and Asquith (1852–1928). Above the statues of these distinguished men is the lovely rose window (1722) designed by Sir James Thornhill. Eleven apostles are depicted; Judas Iscariot has been omitted.

In the north ambulatory, beyond the transept, we see the other side of the tombs of kings and queens in St Edward's Chapel (see page 18). Apart from these the most notable monument is that which commemorates Major General James Wolfe (1727–59) who died heroically in capturing Quebec for the British in 1759. The flags placed on the monument are a lasting reminder of Canada's support for Britain in World War I.

▶ The outer quire screen (1833–34) was designed by the abbey Surveyor, Edward Blore. Within the screen, the 13th-century stonework survives. ⑥

▲ The quire. The eastern side of the quire screen was designed by Sir George Gilbert Scott in 1867. Scott (1811–78), the leading Gothic revivalist, was Surveyor to the abbey from 1849 until his death. He is buried in the nave. ⑬

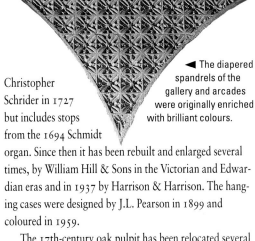

◄ The diapered spandrels of the gallery and arcades were originally enriched with brilliant colours.

The quire was the place in an abbey church where the monks worshipped, usually seven times a day, protected by the screen from the comings and goings of pilgrims and others in the nave. Unfortunately, the 13th-century stalls where the monks of Westminster sat were removed in 1775 when the size of the quire was reduced. The replacement stalls were themselves superseded in 1848 when Edward Blore designed new seating in the Victorian Gothic style.

Today, the daily offices are sung by choirboys from the abbey choir school (usually around 22 in number) and 12 lay vicars (professional choirmen). The organ, since 1730 situated above the quire screen, was originally built by Christopher Schrider in 1727 but includes stops from the 1694 Schmidt organ. Since then it has been rebuilt and enlarged several times, by William Hill & Sons in the Victorian and Edwardian eras and in 1937 by Harrison & Harrison. The hanging cases were designed by J.L. Pearson in 1899 and coloured in 1959.

The 17th-century oak pulpit has been relocated several times in its history, and has in recent years received a pedestal and sounding board.

Under the lantern in the crossing, where quire and sanctuary meet, is the spot where enemy incendiary bombs fell during a World War II air raid. By great good fortune this was perhaps the only place in the abbey where the flames could easily be extinguished. Amazingly, little damage was done then and during other air raids.

The sanctuary, like the quire, has been subject to many changes over the centuries. In medieval times it was adorned with cloth hangings on which were depicted legends of St Edward. These were replaced by wooden panels during the reign of Queen Anne (1702–14). As these hid the fine medieval tombs on the north side they were removed in 1820. The tombs are those of Edmund, Earl of Lancaster and son of Henry III; his wife Aveline; and Aymer de Valence, Earl of Pembroke and cousin of Edward I.

The screen behind the altar was built by monks in the 15th century to separate it from St Edward's shrine beyond, but the magnificent gilded reredos (1873) that we see today was the creation of Sir George Gilbert Scott.

The sedilia, seats for the priests and assistants, were constructed in the time of Edward I. On the sanctuary side, the decoration depicts a saint between two kings. A fourth figure has now disappeared. On the ambulatory side is a

▼ The great pavement in the sanctuary. Completed in 1268 under Abbot Richard de Ware, it was Cosmati work of craftsmen from Rome using Italian materials. ⑭

◀ 'Weepers' from the tomb of Edmund Earl of Lancaster (1245–96). ⑭

Perhaps the greatest treasure of the sanctuary is protected, but sadly concealed, by a carpet. It is the 13th-century great pavement, which bears a mosaic design of porphyries and semi-precious stones, together with an inscription predicting the end of the world. The technique involved is known as Cosmati work and was the creation of craftsmen from Rome.

picture of Edward himself. West of the sedilia is the tomb of Henry VIII's German fourth wife, Anne of Cleves (1515–57). Divorced after a marriage lasting only six months, she lived on in England for another 16 years and was buried here by monks.

The two chairs and faldstools are made of Canadian birch. They were given to the abbey by Canadians in memory of their countrymen killed in World War II.

▼ The exquisite reredos was designed by Sir George Gilbert Scott and erected 1867–73. The figures were sculpted by H.H. Armstead. The mosaic of the Last Supper was designed by J.R. Clayton and executed by A. Salviati. ⑭

▲ A panel from the sedilia, erected in the time of Edward I (reigned 1272–1307). This is possibly the king himself. ⑭

◀ The Coronation of HM Queen Elizabeth II in June 1953. The sovereign sits in the Coronation Chair which is kept in St Edward's Chapel. This part of the ceremony is the Investiture during which the sovereign receives the regalia, the vestments and symbols of regal authority.

▼ The scene at the coronation of George III (reigned 1760–1820).

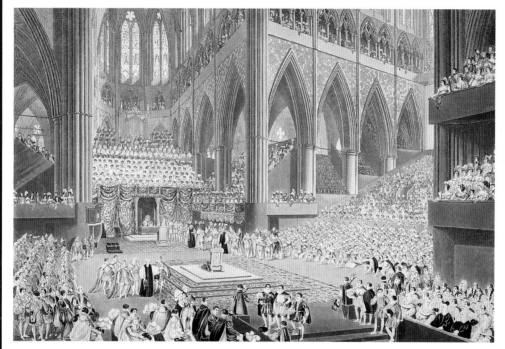

Since William the Conqueror was crowned in Westminster Abbey on Christmas Day 1066, only two monarchs have not been crowned here, Edward V and Edward VIII.

The coronation ceremony is almost certainly very similar to that used in 1066, except that Latin ceased to be used from 1603 onwards. It takes place in the sanctuary, before the high altar, with the sovereign seated on the ancient Coronation Chair. For many centuries the service has been conducted by the Archbishop of Canterbury.

The ceremony has four principal elements within the setting of Holy Communion. In the first part of the service, the sovereign, having been formally accepted by the people, swears an oath promising to rule according to the law and to uphold the Church. Next he or she is anointed with holy oil. Thirdly, after investiture with the royal robes and insignia (the orb and sceptre – symbols of power), comes the actual coronation, when St Edward's crown is placed upon the sovereign's head. Finally, the newly crowned monarch moves to a raised seat beneath the lantern (where quire and sanctuary meet). Here he or she receives homage from the Lords Spiritual and Temporal. After Communion the sovereign processes to the west door and out to meet the cheering crowds.

▲ Monuments to two children of James I, the Princess Sophia (died 1606; cradle) and Mary (1605–7; altar tomb). Both monuments were created by Maximilian Colt, the sculptor of Queen Elizabeth's tomb. ⑲

The eastern aisle of the north transept was formerly three separate chapels, dedicated to St John the Evangelist, St Michael and St Andrew. The whole now tends to be known as the 'Nightingale' Chapel after the splendidly dramatic monument (1761) in the middle bay by L.F. Roubiliac in memory of Lady Elizabeth Nightingale. Her husband Joseph is depicted in stone trying to shield her from the dreaded arrow of death.

The small Jesus Chapel at the west end of the north ambulatory became identified as the chantry chapel for John Islip (Abbot 1500–32), the driving force behind the beautiful Lady Chapel (see page 16) and the completion of the nave. The carving in several places of an eye within a slip, or branch, of a tree and a man slipping from the tree is a rebus, or visual pun, on Islip's name.

The upper part (where the remains of Islip's tomb are now situated) is now a memorial chapel to nurses killed in World War II.

The Chapel of Our Lady of the Pew was formerly a self-contained, highly coloured recess, but now acts as a vestibule to the Chapel of St John the Baptist. In it there stands a modern image of the Virgin and Child based on a 15th-century original. The low vault has a fine roof boss.

The decoration here and on the walls, subdued by time, gives us some idea of the vivid colours that the medieval visitor to Westminster would have seen throughout the abbey.

The Chapel of St John the Baptist contains many fine monuments including one on the north side to Colonel Edward Popham (1610–51), a soldier on the Parliamentary side in the Civil War (1642–49). When Charles II was restored to the throne in 1660, the bodies of most dead Parliamentarians were disinterred and thrown into a pit. But Popham's was carried away, and his monument allowed to stay, on condition that the inscription was erased. In fact the inscribed stone was reversed.

◄ The alabaster statue of Our Lady of the Pew (1971) was carved by Sister Concordia Scott. It was inspired by a 15th-century Madonna now in Westminster Cathedral. ⑰

The next chapel to the east, dedicated to St Paul, is said to have contained the cloth in which St Paul's head was wrapped after his execution – a relic given by Edward the Confessor. Much damage was done to the chapel when a monument to James Watt the inventor, since removed to St Paul's Cathedral, was installed. At the entrance is a monument to Sir Rowland Hill (1795–1879), inventor of the prepaid postal system using stamps, who is buried nearby.

In the north aisle to the Lady Chapel are several notable monuments. Principal among them is the tomb of Queen Elizabeth I who, in 1560, designated the abbey as a collegiate church. Beneath her coffin lies that of her tragic half-sister and predecessor as sovereign, Mary I (reigned 1553–58), known as 'Bloody Mary' for her many executions of Protestants in an attempt to convert the whole of England to Catholicism. By contrast, Elizabeth's reign proved to be a golden age of progress in trade, scholarship and exploration. During this period, stones from broken altars were piled upon Mary's grave.

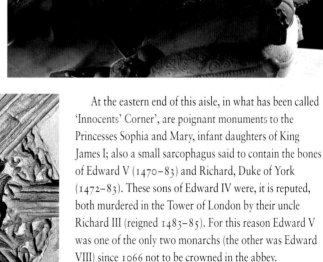

▲ ► The marble tomb of Queen Elizabeth I and her half-sister Mary I was designed by Maximilian Colt and Jean de Critz and erected in 1606 by Queen Elizabeth's successor, James I, at a cost of £765. ⑲

At the eastern end of this aisle, in what has been called 'Innocents' Corner', are poignant monuments to the Princesses Sophia and Mary, infant daughters of King James I; also a small sarcophagus said to contain the bones of Edward V (1470–83) and Richard, Duke of York (1472–83). These sons of Edward IV were, it is reputed, both murdered in the Tower of London by their uncle Richard III (reigned 1483–85). For this reason Edward V was one of the only two monarchs (the other was Edward VIII) since 1066 not to be crowned in the abbey.

◄ A roof boss from the Chapel of Our Lady of the Pew. It is worth examining this and the decorations near it to get a flavour of the highly ornate, brightly painted building that medieval pilgrims would have seen. ⑰

Westminster Abbey from Dean's Yard. The area in the foreground was formerly the farmyard and stables of the abbey. Now two important buildings adjoin it: Westminster School and Church House, administrative centre of the Church of England.

◄ Canaletto's picture of the newly completed west front in 1749 shows the Knights of the Bath processing to the Palace of Westminster after an installation ceremony.

THE LADY CHAPEL (Henry VII's Chapel)

▲ Living Knights of the Bath have a helmet above their stall, often reflecting their interests or their name. ⑳

From the 12th century onward, the Virgin Mary became the subject of particular devotion, and Lady Chapels dedicated to her stand at the east end of almost all of England's great medieval churches. The exquisite Lady Chapel at Westminster was commissioned by Henry VII (reigned 1485–1509). It was built 1503–19 under Abbot Islip in the late Perpendicular style as a replacement for the previous chapel built in 1220. The Tudor king's original idea was to make his peace with God and to provide a suitable burial place for his uncle, Henry VI (reigned 1422–61 and 1470–71) who, he hoped, would be made a saint. But a fitting sum could not be agreed with Rome and Henry VII himself now rests in the splendid tomb behind the altar. Beside him is his wife, Elizabeth of York, whose image to this day appears eight times in every pack of playing cards made.

The chapel's architect is thought to have been Robert Vertue, one of the king's master masons, whose brother William designed similar vaulting for St George's

► The gilded effigies of King Henry VII and his wife, Elizabeth of York. Their tomb, was made by the Florentine artist Pietro Torrigiano. ⑳

◄ The stall plate from the Queen's stall in The Lady Chapel. Each Knight Grand Cross of the Order has one attached to his stall, which remains there in perpetuity. The majority of members of the Order have no stall. ⑳

▼ The RAF Memorial Chapel. Its window includes the insignia of all the squadrons that took part in the Battle of Britain in 1940. Just visible to the left of the altar is a hole, now covered with glass, made by a fragment of a German bomb during the battle. A stone in the floor marks the original burial place of Oliver Cromwell (1599–1658) whose body, with others, was exhumed and violated in 1660. ㉑

Chapel, Windsor at about the same time. Many royal emblems – Tudor roses, fleurs-de-lis, lions, dragons and portcullises – are recurrent in the sumptuous decorations of the chapel. Despite the widespread destruction of painted glass and other fittings at the Reformation, 95 statues of the saints remain of the 107 originals in the niches around the walls.

The royal connection was further strengthened in 1725 when Vertue's creation became the Chapel of the Order of the Bath – the second highest order of chivalry in England, refounded in that year by George I. During the lifetime of each Knight Grand Cross of the Order a stall is appointed for his use, over which his banner is hung and an ornamental helmet placed. An enamelled plaque is placed behind the stall he occupies. On the knight's death, the banners and the helmet go to his next of kin but the stallplates remain in place.

▲ The Lady Chapel. Beneath the altar is the body of Edward VI (reigned 1547–53). The reredos is a 15th-century Madonna and Child by the Venetian artist Bartolommeo Vivarini. ⑳

ST EDWARD'S CHAPEL

St Edward's Chapel is by tradition the focus of the abbey, for it contains what was once its greatest wonder, the tomb of the founder, King (later Saint) Edward the Confessor. Edward, who ruled 1042–66, was famed for his asceticism and piety. He was originally buried by the altar of the 11th-century church but, after miracles took place there, William I commissioned a fine tomb, gilded and jewelled. This became an object of national reverence and pilgrimage.

Henry III in his reconstruction of the abbey had an even more impressive tomb constructed. A golden shrine (feretory) containing the Confessor's coffin was placed on a base of Purbeck 'marble' and mosaic, surrounded by a pavement of Italian porphyries. Above was a movable canopy. The feretory was decorated with gold images of kings and saints. Two gilded statues, of St Edward and St John the Evangelist, stood on pillars at the side, and an altar was erected at the west end of the chapel. On 13 October 1269, Henry III, his brother and two sons carried St Edward's

▼ The tomb effigy of Henry III, who built the present Westminster Abbey. ㉔

coffin in procession to its new resting place.

In 1540 the monastic community, which had been at Westminster for nearly 600 years, was dissolved by order of King Henry VIII. The shrine, as were so many others throughout the land, was robbed of its relics and seriously damaged. The body in its coffin was removed and buried elsewhere. In 1557, under Henry's daughter Mary I, the shrine was rebuilt rather clumsily. The jewels were replaced and, as there was no feretory, the coffin was restored to the top part of the stone base. The next 100 years saw several acts of vandalism and theft. In 1685 after King James II's coronation, a choirman, Charles Taylour, removed

◀ The tomb of Edward the Confessor (1269), once a visual feast of gold and gilt encrusted with jewels and mosaic. Since 1540, only the base remains of the original. The recesses are where pilgrims knelt to pray. ㉔

▶ Pilgrims at the original shrine of Edward the Confessor.

a gold cross and chain having seen it glint through a hole in the coffin. Having handed it in, he received £50 from the king for his initiative and honesty. After that, a surrounding coffin was constructed and fastened with iron bands. Since then the body has rested undisturbed.

Among others buried in the chapel are Henry III (reigned 1216–72) who rebuilt the abbey, his son Edward I (reigned 1272–1307; nicknamed 'Longshanks') and his wife Eleanor of Castile. Eleanor died in Nottinghamshire. In transporting her body to Westminster Abbey, Edward had monuments ('crosses') constructed wherever the procession rested overnight. Charing Cross in London is the final one of these. Richard II and Edward III with their queens are also buried in St Edward's Chapel.

At the west end is a 15th-century stone screen depicting events, real and legendary, of the Confessor's life. Against it stands the Coronation Chair. Formerly gilded and encrusted with sparkling glass and enamels, this ancient witness to a nation's history has been subjected to many acts of vandalism through the ages, not least in the 18th century, when boys of the choir school were allowed to roam free in the abbey. Beneath the chair is the Stone of Scone (pronounced 'scoon'), the ancient coronation seat of early Scottish kings. Edward I seized it from the Scots in 1296 and it has remained here since, defying all attempts to reclaim it; this despite being stolen for a brief period in 1950–51 by Scottish Nationalists.

▶ The Coronation Chair, which stands before the high altar during coronation ceremonies. Beneath is the Stone of Scone, ancient coronation chair of Scottish kings, weighing 208kg (458lbs). ㉔

At the east end of St Edward's Chapel is the Chantry Chapel of Henry V (reigned 1413–22), who is famed in particular for his victory over the French at Agincourt in 1415, immortalized in Shakespeare's play. The chantry was built in the medieval tradition so that masses could be said for the dead king's soul. Henry's tomb of polished Purbeck stone, traditionally one of the great sights of the abbey, has lost much of its splendour. In 1546, after the dissolution of the monastery, the king's effigy was rendered headless and the silver regalia stolen. The head we see today is a replica dating from 1971.

▲ The effigy of Mary Queen of Scots who, after her execution in 1687, was initially buried at Peterborough Cathedral. Her son, James I, had her remains brought to Westminster in the early 17th century. ㉒

The south aisle of the Lady Chapel is dominated by three elaborate tombs. The farthest monument is that of Lady Margaret Beaufort, Henry VII's mother. Her effigy by Pietro Torrigiano is one of the finest in the abbey. The nearest tomb to the aisle entrance commemorates Margaret, Countess of Lennox (1515–78), the beautiful niece of Henry VIII and grandmother to James I. She died in poverty at Hackney, London. King James erected the tomb after his succession in 1603.

The central tomb is that of Mary Queen of Scots (1542–87) whose first husband was Henry, Lord Darnley, son of the Countess of Lennox mentioned above. A devout Roman Catholic and a claimant to the English throne, Mary posed a severe threat to the Protestant Queen Elizabeth I. She was captured and imprisoned for 19 years at

► The male 'weepers' on the tomb of Margaret, Countess of Lennox (1515–78). Foremost is her son Henry, Lord Darnley (1545–67), husband of Mary Queen of Scots and father of James I, who helped to murder Mary's secretary Rizzio and who was himself killed a year later. ㉒

Fotheringhay Castle in Northamptonshire, only to be executed in 1587. Originally buried in Peterborough Cathedral, Mary's remains were brought to the abbey by her son, James I. The tomb was sculpted by William and Cornelius Cure.

Many of James's successors are buried here in Queen Mary's vault or in the royal vault below. These include Charles II (reigned 1660–85), joint sovereigns William III (reigned 1689–1702) and Mary II (reigned 1689–94), and Queen Anne (reigned 1702–14).

In the south ambulatory, one can see the other side of Edward III's tomb. Especially lovely is the line of bronze 'weepers', the term often used to describe images along the side of a tomb of the kneeling sons and

daughters of the deceased. Also nearby is a retable (a panel showing a painted image) of Christ in Glory which dates from about 1270.

The three chapels in this area of the abbey, those dedicated to St Nicholas, St Edmund and St Benedict, all contain exquisite and ornate monuments commemorating members of the nobility and clergy, notably those from the 16th and 17th century. The 13th-century heraldic glass in St Edmund's Chapel is of particular interest, as is the tomb of William de Valence, which is the only existing example of Limoges enamelwork on a tomb in England.

▼ The effigy of Lady Margaret Beaufort, mother of Henry VII, by Pietro Torrigiano. ㉒

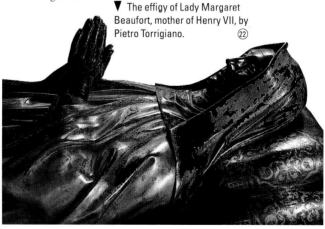

THE SOUTH TRANSEPT AND POETS' CORNER

▲ The tomb of the great poet Geoffrey Chaucer (*c.*1343–1400), who lived in the shadow of the abbey in a cottage that was knocked down to make way for the building of Henry VII's Chapel. ㉙

I n Westminster Abbey, the burial of one person eminent in a particular field has led to others of the same calling choosing to be buried nearby. The monument to Isaac Newton led to a cluster of scientists in the north aisle; William Pitt was the first of many statesmen to be commemorated by a statue in the north transept.

It was the tombs of the poets Geoffrey Chaucer and Edmund Spenser that led to the south transept becoming a popular resting-place for poets and dramatists – hence the nickname 'Poets' Corner'.

Around 1550, Chaucer's body was moved from near the adjacent St Benedict's Chapel to a tomb erected by Nicholas Brigham, a minor poet. Spenser, author of *The Faerie Queene*, was buried in 1599 at a funeral

▼ The tablet marking the grave of Thomas Parr – who died in 1635 at the reputed age of 152. Many overseas visitors like to touch it in the hope of achieving similar longevity. ㉙

▲ The rose window in the south transept. Its tracery was remodelled in 1849–50 by Sir George Gilbert Scott, Surveyor to the abbey, and the glass replaced in 1901 as a memorial to the 1st Duke of Westminster. ㉙

THO: PARR OF Y COUNTY OF SALLOP BORNE IN A: 1483. HE LIVED IN y REIGNES OF TEN PRINCES VIZ: K. EDW. 4. K. ED. 5. K. RICH. 3. K. HEN. 7. K. HEN. 8. K. EDW. 6. Q. MA. Q. ELIZ. K. JA. & K. CHARLES. AGED 152 YEARES. & WAS BURYED HERE NOVEMB. 15. 1635.

One of the often unnoticed treasures of the abbey – a censing angel in stone from the south transept. (29)

Robert Adam and composer George Frederick Handel. Handel's imposing statue by L.F. Roubiliac is reputed to be an exact likeness. Above here is the Muniment Room which houses the abbey's archive collection.

A tablet near the south-east door of the transept reminds us that William Caxton, in 1476, set up England's first printing press nearby. Also at the end of the south transept is the small Chapel of St Faith, which is reserved for private prayer and meditation.

▼ A bronze bust of the poet William Blake created in 1957 by the eminent sculptor Sir Jacob Epstein. (29)

attended by most of his great literary contemporaries, probably including William Shakespeare. All of the mourners wrote elegies and threw them, with the pens, into the grave.

Famous writers buried in the abbey include Francis Beaumont, Robert Browning, Charles Dickens, John Dryden, Thomas Hardy, Dr Johnson, Ben Jonson, Rudyard Kipling, Lord Macaulay, John Masefield, Richard Brinsley Sheridan and Alfred, Lord Tennyson.

Other people from the field of arts and music interred here include actors Garrick, Irving and Olivier, architect

In modern times Westminster Abbey has become a
living memorial to the history of the nation, but in
the first five centuries of its life, things were very
different. The title 'abbey' survives from the Middle
Ages when the church we know today was the centre
of worship for a Benedictine monastery.

At any one time, between 30 and 60 monks lived at
Westminster, with up to 300 other people involved in the
day-to-day running of the monastery. Although not the
largest, Westminster Abbey was the wealthiest in Britain
because of its royal patronage. Monks followed the Rule
of St Benedict, a gently demanding way of life – attending
services during the day and night, reading, writing and

◀ The remarkable flying buttresses supporting the nave are
a distinctively French element of Henry de Reyns' design.

◀ The cloister was the focal point of the medieval monastery, a place for quiet reflection and for study. (34)

gardening. They may also have had to travel to attend to one of the 216 manors owned by the monastery elsewhere in England.

Many of the younger monks went to Oxford to study, while many of the senior ones had a well-defined role in the running of the monastery, with titles such as almoner, cellarer, guest master and so on. Elderly monks would be likely to end their days in the infirmary, located where the Little Cloister still stands.

In medieval times, the abbot of a monastery wielded very considerable power, not only over the monks, who were subject to vows of obedience, but also over the estates and subsidiary religious houses owned by the monastery. He had legal powers also, for abbeys held courts to try local wrong-doers. Many abbots lived separately in splendid households with dozens of servants. Often the king would send an abbot on important diplomatic missions.

Many parts of Westminster's ancient monastery survived the Dissolution and can be seen today. The abbey garden is believed to be one of the oldest in England, having been under continuous cultivation for over 900 years. The abbey's farmyard and stables occupied the open space now known as Dean's Yard.

Several monastic buildings still exist, including the dormitory (now the abbey library), the abbot's lodging, the cellarer's range (wine and provision store), the Chapter House (see page 26) and, central to it all, the cloister.

This covered walk had many functions – a passageway, a route for processions, a place for meditation. Young novices and children from outside were taught at stone benches in the west walk. Older monks read or wrote in carrels (cubicles for study) in the north walk. Perhaps on another side, the maundy, a regular ritual foot-washing, was carried out. Books were stored in recesses or cupboards around the walls, which were painted and hung with pictures. Originally, only the upper parts of the window bays were glazed, with wooden screens and leather curtains elsewhere in an attempt to keep draughts out. Working areas were carpeted with hay, straw or rush mats for warmth and quiet. At night the cloister was lit by lamps.

In 1540 Abbot Boston signed a deed of surrender in the Chapter House and the monastery at Westminster ceased to exist. Many priceless treasures were sold off to bolster Henry VIII's depleted finances. There was much destruction. Queen Mary's reign saw a brief attempt to revive the Benedictine community, but after the accession of Elizabeth I the monks left the cloister, this time for ever.

◀ A passage beneath the former monks' dormitory leads to the Little Cloister, a charming garden within a square of houses built for clergy of the abbey. (34)

THE CHAPTER HOUSE & PYX CHAMBER

The Chapter House was where monastic business was conducted, important guests received and often, in early times, where superiors were buried. The chapter, the monks' daily conference, took place there. After Mass, the monks processed to the Chapter House. There they prayed for the dead and for their benefactors. A monk would read aloud a chapter of the Benedictine Rule, which is how the meeting got its name. The abbot or his delegate often then gave a sermon or commentary. The day's business followed – notices, correspondence, duties, reports, etc. There might then be a choir practice or rehearsal particularly if an important service was imminent.

▼ The Chapter House. Some of the glass dates from Sir George Gilbert Scott's restoration 1866–72, which revealed medieval encaustic floor tiles in excellent condition. On the walls are early 15th-century paintings, including a scene of the Last Judgement. ㉛

Finally monastic discipline was discussed. Any breaches of the Rule were brought to light and a superior would decree punishment. Often the offending monk was beaten with a rod or bundle of sticks. The Rule dictated that during this 'all the brethren should bow down with a kind and brotherly compassion'.

Westminster's Chapter House is the second largest in England (after Lincoln), reflecting its national importance, for from its completion in 1253 until 1547 it was one of the regular meeting places of Parliament. Since the Reformation the Chapter House has belonged to the Crown, not the abbey. It only survived the ravages of dissolution because it was used to house royal records, which it did until 1863. During its three centuries as a store it suffered ravages of a different kind: the windows were blocked, an internal gallery built and – final insult – in 1744 the vault was destroyed and a new floor inserted, resting on the central pillar.

Sir George Gilbert Scott between 1866 and 1872 returned some parts to their original appearance but other details, such as the steep roof, owed more to his own fancy than to medieval reality.

Next to the Chapter House is an ancient room with a massive double door. This was once a chapel, but in the 14th century it became the monastic treasury. This followed a daring raid in 1303 on the former treasury beneath the Chapter House by one Richard de Podelicote, aided and abetted by certain monks, later sent to the Tower.

The Pyx Chamber, guarded by six locks, was used mainly by the Exchequer to house the coronation regalia, money in transit and important documents. A pyx in this context means the strong box that contained the 'trial plates', the nation's standard pieces of gold and silver. Each year, current coins were tested for purity against these, before a jury made up mainly of goldsmiths. This exercise was known as the 'Trial of the Pyx'.

Since 1986 the chamber very appropriately has housed the fine collection of silver plate – mainly chalices, plates and flagons belonging to the abbey and its associated

church, St Margaret's, Westminster. This dates from the 16th century onward, as all the medieval plate disappeared either during the Reformation or the Commonwealth, when the monarchy was overthrown. Also on display is a curved medieval chest for storing copes, the large cloaks used by priests on ceremonial occasions. The golden cope within was possibly made for the coronation of Charles II in 1661.

◀ A 17th-century communion plate on display in the Pyx Chamber. ㉜

▼ The Pyx Chamber before adaption to its present use. It was first a chapel and then a storehouse for the state. ㉜

Today, as it has done for the last 900 years, Westminster Abbey plays a central role in the life of the United Kingdom and its Commonwealth. It is in this church above all others where the British people come before God in celebration or in mourning. Every year, with dignity and ceremony, the abbey bears witness to Britain's unfolding history. An enormous range of special services is held here – celebrations of Commonwealth countries, commemorations of important anniversaries, remembrances of figures of national importance and, of course, the splendid royal occasions that are watched by the world.

Many events are part of the abbey's regular calendar. Every four years new Knights of the Bath are installed. Every ten years the sovereign distributes the Royal Maundy here, a symbolic commemoration of Christ washing his disciples' feet.

It is important to remember that, despite its significance as principal church to the nation, the abbey has a no less essential daily role. It is wonderful to consider that worship has taken place here every day for well over 900 years. Each weekday sees at least three services and on Sundays there are usually five or more. When, during the day, there is no service in progress, a clergyman enters the nave pulpit once an hour to remind visitors by a minute

▲ The lesson is read during the service held in the abbey in July 1994 to celebrate the return of South Africa to the Commonwealth.

▼ Archbishop Desmond Tutu and Bishop Trevor Huddleston enjoy a happy moment at the west door of the abbey after the service pictured above.

◄ The abbey choir is internationally famous for the quality of its singing. The abbey has its own choir school which is unique in that it is run exclusively for the boys of the choir.

► Back cover: The nave viewed from the quire screen, looking towards the west door.

of prayer that the abbey is far more than an historic monument. In addition there are two chapels, St George's and St Faith's, set aside for prayer or quiet meditation.

The abbey has a long-standing and proud reputation for the excellence of its music. The choir consists of 12 men and the 22 senior boys of the Westminster Abbey Choir School, a unique establishment which is run by the Dean and Chapter specifically for boys of the choir.

Although its fabric demands constant attention, Westminster Abbey is a thriving and active church. By the grace of God and the efforts of men and women, this unique church will continue to hold its place in the hearts and minds of the nation for many centuries more.

For further information
(times of services etc) contact:
The Chapter Office,
Westminster Abbey,
20 Dean's Yard,
London, SW1P 3PA.
Telephone 0171-222-5152

Acknowledgements

The publishers wish to acknowledge the kind assistance of Emma St John-Smith, Dr Richard Mortimer, Dr Tony Trowles and English Heritage in the preparation of this book.

Written and edited by John McIlwain.

Designed by John Buckley.

All photographs are © Pitkin Pictorials (by Angelo Hornak, Mark Fiennes and Peter Smith of Newbery Smith Photography) except for:

Hulton Deutsch: p.11 top.
Michael Holford: p.3 bottom.
Angelo Hornak: p.19 bottom.
Ian Jones: p.28 top.
Peter Orme: p.28 bottom.
Westminster Abbey: p.9, p.28 (photograph by John Crook).
Cambridge University Library: p.19 top.

The painting on page 2 is reproduced by kind permission of the City of Westminster.

The pictures on pages 1 (top), 11, 15 (inset) are reproduced by kind permission of the Dean and Chapter of Westminster.

Publication in this form © Pitkin Pictorials 1995

Printed in Great Britain.
ISBN 0 85372 727 9

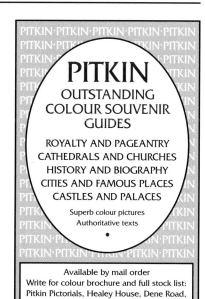

9 780853 727279 >